NOTE TO SELF

CHAPTER

I

WRITTEN BY

CHIDOZIE E. OSUWA

outskirts
press

Outskirts Press, Inc.
http://www.outskirtspress.com

ISBN: 978-1-9772-1578-9

PRINTED IN THE UNITED STATES OF AMERICA

<u>Note to self:</u>
How they treat you is more important than how much you like them.
12:34 AM.

Stop allowing your attraction to someone cause you to ignore how they treat you. It should always take precedence. Someone you like is not hard to find. Someone who values you is.

<u>Note to self:</u>
My respect is not up for negotiation.
1:23 PM.

Yes, there should be compromise in relationships. But respect should not be one of them. That should come standard with anyone. It is simply the minimum.

<u>Note to self:</u>
Love is not enough for me. It must come with loyalty.
7:23 PM.

Honestly, if it doesn't come with loyalty, I can hardly call it love. Not my kind of love, anyways. It is way too easy for people to throw that word "love" around. A lot harder for them to prove it... consistently.

<u>Note to self:</u>
Be unapologetic about knowing what you will not put up with.
2:12 AM.

Don't apologize for having standards. Don't apologize for knowing what you want and what you don't want. You deserve what makes you happy. And you deserve someone who is willing to do those things.

<u>Note to self:</u>
The qualities you need may not be wrapped in a package you are used to.
4:56 PM.

You may want to consider dating outside of your "type" at some point. Sometimes, what you think you want may be in the way of what you need. Those restrictions you have in place may just be what are blocking you from your blessing. I'm not saying you have to date someone that you are not attracted to. I'm saying you should be open. Don't limit yourself.

<u>Note to self:</u>
Not everyone that applies gets an interview; let alone, the position.
8:34 PM.

Have a "screening process", in a sense. Stop giving people important roles in your life before really getting to know them. People aren't always what they seem. Too often we rush things because of lust, or a physical attraction. We trick our minds into believing someone is "the one" because we want them to be.

<u>Note to self:</u>
Life is too short to spend pretending you're happy when you're not.
3:14 PM.

Make sure you are actually happy in your relationship; and if you're not, speak up, or make changes. Our time on earth is limited. You should do your best to spend it being happy with people who bring out the best in you.

<u>Note to self:</u>
I will not base my happiness on who chooses to love me.
9:23 AM

You don't have to be in a relationship to be happy. Find happiness within you. Your time single shouldn't be spent just waiting (for love). It should be spent finding you, loving yourself, and living!

<u>Note to self:</u>
**Stop giving blind loyalty to people who aren't committing back to you.
3:08 PM.**

Everyone doesn't deserve loyalty. Make sure they earn it. Make sure it's reciprocated. Make sure you're not just giving it away for free.

<u>Note to self:</u>
I will reserve my unconditional love for those who have shown me they are deserving of it, because they have my best interest at heart at all times.
7:34 PM.

Only people who have proven time and time again that they are for you deserve your unconditional love. And even then, it doesn't mean that you must let that person walk all over you. It means that you love them through their good and bad times. You are still allowed to distant yourself from people you love "unconditionally" for the sake of your own well-being.

__Note to self:__
When a man tells you he is not ready, believe him.
2:54 AM.

Stop trying to force men to want what you want when you want it. You are setting yourself up for disappointment. A lot of men may not even give you the courtesy of telling you up front what they are or are not ready for. Some will lead you on to get whatever it is they want from you. So, when a man does have the courage to tell you what he is not ready for, do yourself a favor, and believe him.

<u>Note to self:</u>
I will not convince myself that people are something other than what they show me.
3:21 AM.

Stop turning a blind eye to who a person is because of who your attraction to them has made them out to be in your head. It's ok to see peoples potential. Not ok to completely ignore their reality.

<u>Note to self:</u>
Stop holding on to people who have shown you they do not value the relationship.
5:12 PM

A relationship cannot work when only one person values it. You shouldn't be acting taken while your partner is acting single. That's not a relationship. That's manipulation.

<u>Note to self:</u>
I will love myself enough to say fuck anything and anyone that isn't bringing me peace or happiness.
9:23 PM

Anything that jeopardizes your peace or happiness must go. The point of relationships is to add to your peace and happiness, not take away from them.

<u>Note to self:</u>
I will no longer try to teach adults how to be adults.
7:23 PM

At a certain age, you shouldn't have to be raising someone while trying to date them. It's draining; and it's not your job. If he still needs to be raised, send his ass back to his mother.

Note to self:
Stop begging people for effort. They either want to give it, or they don't.
9:53 PM

Anyone you have to beg for time or effort is simply not it. Let go. Move on.

<u>Note to self:</u>
Let go of memories of what used to be, and accept the reality of what is.
2:42 AM.

Don't let who someone was years ago keep you prisoner to their current bullshit, and disrespect. Relationships should not only be good in the beginning. You don't have any obligation to stay in relationships that are unhealthy. There should always be effort. There should always be love. There should always be respect.

<u>Note to self:</u>
I will no longer allow people to use "our history" to pull me back into their bullshit. 8:56 AM.

Learn that "history" works against you a lot of times. It plays into your comfort with that person, even when you know they are toxic or no good for you. It's ok to start over. Stop running back to what you know just because it's what you know.

<u>Note to self:</u>
Put a limit on how many chances you give people. Put a limit on how many apologies you accept from the same person for the same shit.
3:53 PM.

Those unlimited chances you keep giving people will have you stuck in the same predicament and wasting years of your life. Stop it. Nothing changes when they know they will always have "one more chance".

<u>Note to self:</u>
Stop expecting everyone to love the way you do. However, don't be blind and keep pouring into people who are not pouring back into you.
2:44 PM.

Not everyone loves like you. To expect that from everyone you meet or date is unreasonable. However, make sure the way they love is compatible with the way you want and need to be loved. Make sure it pours into your soul. Make sure they are able and willing to learn your love language.

Note to self:
I will not keep fighting for people who won't even show up to the ring.
9:23 PM.

We have to learn to stop going so hard for people who don't do the same for us. You shouldn't always be the one trying to fix the relationship, or rectify an issue. If they are never the one to take the initiative, then that speaks to their lack of value for you or the relationship.

<u>Note to self:</u>
Stop waiting for that call or text, and carry on with your life as they have with theirs. 8:23 AM.

They have already used up enough of your time with that failed relationship. Don't waste anymore waiting for them... move on.

<u>Note to self:</u>
Stop being afraid to let go of people who are not afraid to let go of you.
2:44 AM.

Sometimes, the best thing you can do is truly understand the nature of the relationship you have with someone, and the way they feel about you. That way, you don't over-value your role in their life, and their role in yours.

<u>Note to self:</u>
Stop letting that excitement of something new cause you to open up so easily and fall so quickly.
4:19 AM.

We all love a new spark. But remember to still keep your guards up. Remember to still pay attention to red flags. Remember to still take the time to get to know that person. Don't let those new and exciting feelings cause you to rush.

<u>Note to self:</u>
Stop telling yourself that you deserve better and then settling for whatever is available at the time.
1:47 PM.

Wait for the love you want. Wait for the love you know that you deserve. To know your worth and continuously settle for less is just as bad, if not worse, than not even knowing your worth in the first place. You know better. Now, do better!

Note to self:
Stop making permanent plans for temporary people. 11:44 AM.

Not everyone that comes into your life intends to be there for the long run. Know this and act accordingly. Stop changing your entire life for people who may be gone before you know it.

<u>Note to self:</u>
Stop letting "potential" be the reason you keep allowing yourself to be mistreated over and over again.
9:18 AM.

There is nothing wrong with seeing the potential in someone. However, no relationship should be based on potential, alone. Not everyone sees in themselves the potential that you might. Some people don't even care for that potential. You can't continuously allow yourself to be mistreated because you are hoping that, someday, that person will realize the same potential that you do, and decide to change their behavior for the better. That is a sure way to set yourself up for disappointment.

<u>Note to self:</u>
Stop allowing boredom to guide you back to misery. 5:54 PM.

Find an activity to keep your mind off them. Learn to be alone. It's hard, but healing is a process that you interrupt every time you allow yourself to go back to what keeps breaking you.

<u>Note to self:</u>
Stop accepting apologies that do not come with changed behavior.
2:32 AM.

Apologies that do not come with changed behavior are simply manipulation techniques. Stop allowing it. Anyone who isn't following up their apology with change is not sorry.

<u>Note to self:</u>
Forgive him, but deny his access.
4:53 PM

Learn to forgive toxic people but still distance yourself. Forgiveness doesn't mean you have to keep giving them the opportunity to damage you.

<u>Note to self:</u>
I will not be their peace, when all they bring me is chaos.
5:27 PM.

Understand that just as much as their peace matters to them, yours matters, too! You deserve someone who can reciprocate everything that they require.

<u>Note to self:</u>
Stop continuing to make time for people who have continued to waste it.
7:33 AM.

Once someone shows you that they do not value your time, accept that. Time is the most valuable asset we have in life. You can't get it back. So, make people earn your time. Make people earn you.

<u>Note to self:</u>
Leave his inconsistent ass on 'read'.
4:44 AM

Not everyone deserves a response. Especially inconsistent people who only use you to pass time. You are more than that.

<u>Note to self:</u>
Learn to stop waiting for an apology that you may never receive, or closure that may never be offered.
9:17 PM.

Sometimes, you'll have to just move on... without an apology; without an explanation. Sometimes, you have to decide that you don't even need it. You have to decide that you don't even need to know WHY they fucked you over, and that the fact THAT they fucked you over is all you really need to know.

<u>Note to self:</u>

Don't stop being a good person, but be mindful and more careful with the people you choose to invest your energy in.

6:28 AM.

It's so tempting to want to change and start treating people how you feel like you have been treated in the past. I urge you not to. Don't become them. Just be more careful with the kind of people you allow in your space. You will eventually attract the kind of people who reciprocate your kind of energy.

<u>Note to self:</u>
Stop making excuses to stay in a toxic situation. 4:37 AM.

Too many times we make excuses for people we love because it's hard to walk away. Those excuses become less for them, and more so for you; to excuse your lack of courage to do what needs to be done. Be strong. Save yourself.

<u>Note to self:</u>
Do not lose yourself chasing anyone.
8:19 AM.

Simply put, no one is worth that.

NO ONE.

<u>Note to self:</u>
Remember to love yourself. Even while loving someone else.
3:50 PM.

It's easy to get lost in someone. Especially when you feel a heavy attraction to that person. However, it's important to remember to still take care of yourself, mentally, physically, and emotionally.

<u>Note to self:</u>
Stop allowing yourself to be treated less than you deserve because you are afraid of starting over.
6:17 AM.

Comfort is one of the most dangerous things. Too often, people stay in toxic situations because it's what they know or because starting over terrifies them. Don't be that person. Starting over won't kill you. And just because you're comfortable somewhere does not mean that is where you belong.

<u>Note to self:</u>
You never stop being responsible for your own happiness.
4:27 AM.

The goal is not to meet someone and give them the responsibility of making you happy. That never stops being your job. The goal should be for them to add to your happiness; to add to your peace.

<u>Note to self:</u>
Fall in love with people, not the idea of who you want them to be.
2:14 PM

Too often, we meet someone we are attracted to, and then create this fantasy in our minds of who they are, and fall in love with that. Learn to take the time to get to know people, and fall in love with them, not that idea.

<u>Note to self:</u>
Stop reaching out to toxic people you claim to be leaving behind. Leave them there.
8:29 PM.

One of the most important things you can learn when attempting to heal or move on is to stop looking back.

<u>Note to self:</u>
If they aren't making time and putting in effort on their own free will, let them go. 2:12 PM.

Don't try to control anyone. Don't try to pressure anyone to give you effort. You will see how they truly feel by what they choose to do on their own.

<u>Note to self:</u>
Having reasonable adult expectations is not asking for too much. Stay away from people who think it is.
7:08 AM

Those who say you're asking for too much are usually those who have low effort, and know it.

<u>Note to self:</u>
Be selective with who you give your time to, because once feelings get involved, it becomes harder to pull away.
1:34 PM

Be cautious with who you invest your time with. Sometimes, you can tell within the first few interactions with someone what kind of person they are. Learn to trust your gut.

<u>Note to self:</u>
Stop being afraid to wait for your blessing alone. It's coming.
6:48 AM.

Master the art of being alone. Not only will it help you find yourself, it will keep you from settling for any bullshit that comes your way that you know is not what you want.

<u>Note to self:</u>
Keep living your life. By the time they realize what they missed out on, it won't even matter. You'll be out of reach and unavailable.
5:18 AM.

Don't stop your life for anyone. Keep going. The people you are supposed to cross paths with will meet you. The people who are supposed to remain in your life will find a way to do so.

<u>Note to self:</u>
Some relationships will have an expiration date. learn to be ok with that.
3:02 PM.

Learn to be ok with when friendships and/or relationships run their course. Sometimes, You'll simply outgrow people.

<u>Note to self:</u>
Sex is not and never should be more important than how you're treated.
4:23 AM.

Not saying that sex isn't and shouldn't be an important factor in your relationship. What I am saying is that sex isn't hard to find. Even good sex can be taught. But teaching someone to value you, is a much harder task.

<u>Note to self:</u>
Just because you miss them does not mean you need to give them access back into your life.
5:23 PM.

It's possible and actually common to miss someone that you know is no good for you. That's not a sign that you need to go back or reconnect with them. It's only a sign that you are human. Stay away. Don't interrupt your healing process. Miss them until you don't anymore.

Note to self:
Just because he shows you different doesn't mean he's different.
People are good at pretending. Give it time to know the real person.
5:25 AM.

I pray you meet someone who is everything they show you in the beginning. Time will show you whether or not you did. Watch their actions and their habits over time.

<u>Note to self:</u>
If your emotional and spiritual needs are not being equally met or prioritized as much as your sexual needs, you may want to rethink that relationship.
6:08 PM.

Sex is great, but a relationship should be more than that. If that's all a person has to offer you, it won't last. Make sure they care about all of you and not just how you can make them feel in bed.

<u>Note to self:</u>
You don't have to explain your standards to anyone. Men who look to complain about them should look somewhere else for someone they can handle. 8:43 AM.

You're not for everybody, and you have to learn to be ok with that. Don't let anyone bully you into settling or second-guessing your standards.

Note to self:
Stop pretending nothing is wrong so that you can continue to remain in a failing relationship. Speak up! If they're not looking to fix the problems, then perhaps it's time you let go. 9:12 PM.

<u>Note to self:</u>
Stop giving people these huge roles in your before they have proven themself. Make them work for it.
8:34 AM

Make sure people feel the same about you as you feel about them. Make sure they actually want that role in your life before you give it to them in your head.

<u>Note to self:</u>
**Stop letting temporary feelings for temporary people stand in the way of what you say you want. Make room for your blessing.
6:42 PM.**

Some people are meant to be temporary. When you realize this about someone, make sure you do not let them stand in the way of something that could be more long term.

<u>Note to self:</u>
**Stop being a wife to a dude who can't even be a faithful boyfriend.
1:34 PM.**

**Treat people according to who they are.
Your boyfriend is not your husband.
Don't rush and skip steps.**

<u>Note to self:</u>
You shouldn't be still trying to teach a grown man what loyalty means. If he's showing you that he's not willing to be that, accept that truth, and move along. 7:17 PM.

Most people know what it means to be loyal. They are either incapable of being that, or don't want to be that to you. Either way, you need to accept one of those truths and move on.

<u>Note to self:</u>
Sometimes, you'll grow out of people, and it's not your fault. The goal is someone who can grow with you, not someone who will make you feel bad for progressing. 8:49 AM.

<u>Note to self:</u>
Don't forget about your own mental health.
6:16 AM.

While you're out there trying to save everyone else, don't forget about yourself.

Note to self:

Be strong enough to reject anything less than what you know you deserve. Stop letting people give you whatever it is they feel like giving you when you know it's not what you want or need. 5:57 AM.

<u>Note to self:</u>
Don't forget to update your block list.
3:41 PM.

Revoke people's access to you as often as needed. You don't owe anyone anything; especially people who add nothing positive to your life. You are in control.

<u>Note to self:</u>
Before you send that long ass text to address some fuck shit he knows he did, but refuses to openly admit, ask yourself if it's even worth it.
9:54 AM.

Not every relationship is worth saving. Not everything is worth addressing. A lot of times, people know what they did, they just don't want to own it.

<u>Note to self:</u>
Being a real woman is not about how much bullshit you can take from a man. 4:22 AM.

Don't let anyone convince you that a good woman is defined by how much bullshit you tolerate. The men who would have you believe that are the same ones who don't define a "good man" by how much disrespect he tolerates. Don't let anyone convince you that you should be putting up with things that they themselves would not even consider putting up with.

<u>Note to self:</u>
Stop prioritizing people who are not prioritizing you. Sometimes, you need to be unavailable until their effort proves them worthy of your time.
6:44 PM.

<u>Note to self:</u>
Don't let your desire to be in love cause you to fall for anything
4:11 AM.

When you love love, or yearn for it so much, it's easy to rush into situations. Take your time. Learn people. Make sure it's love, and not just lust, or desperation, or just the desire to have someone around.

<u>Note to self:</u>
Stop investing energy
in anyone you have to
convince of your worth.
8:32 AM.

<u>Note to self:</u>
That potential you see means nothing if he himself doesn't see it, or want to reach it.
2:35 PM.

A man who isn't trying to realize his potential is a man who's potential becomes irrelevant.

<u>Note to self:</u>
Stop committing to people who are only giving you half effort.
6:37 PM.

Stop giving all of you to people who are only giving you bits of them whenever they feel like it. You'll always feel drained. Make sure it's equal on both sides.

<u>Note to self:</u>
**Keep your standards high. It will at least filter away some of the fuck boys.
4:07 PM.**

Yes, men will still try their hand. Fuck-boys will still try their hand. But at least the ones who think your standards are too high might be discouraged from even approaching you.

<u>Note to self:</u>
Just because you like someone does not mean they deserve you.
6:52 PM.

Liking someone is not enough. Make sure they are worth your time and effort. Make sure your energy is reciprocated. Make sure they know how to love you correctly.

<u>Note to self:</u>
You're always asking for too much to the "men" who know they can't play with you.
9:19 AM.

<u>Note to self:</u>
Let go of your fear of starting over.
8:09 PM.

<u>Note to self:</u>
Sometimes, you need to let go of your need for closure. Because sometimes, when you're trying to shut that door, it's that need for an explanation that keeps it open and continues to give that toxic person access to you that they should not have.
1:52 PM.

Stop waiting for an explanation. It's holding you back. I don't know who or what convinced you that you need one in order to move on… you don't.

<u>Note to self:</u>
Stop entertaining "lets just see where it goes" type of dudes.
5:55 PM.

A man who wants you is sure and will make it known. Anyone else is probably about to waste your time.

<u>Note to self:</u>
You deserve consistency without having to beg.
3:31 PM.

<u>Note to self:</u>
Give yourself time to heal.
7:19 PM.

Do not jump into relationships just to fill a void. It's not fair to you, or your partner.

<u>Note to self:</u>
Be with someone who is loyal to you when your back is turned.
5:04 AM.

The best way to judge character is by how your partner represents you when you're not watching them. Anyone can be on their best behavior when you're around.

<u>Note to self:</u>
Stop expecting time to heal you when you are so hell bent on holding on.
2:17 AM.

If you truly want to heal, you'll have to understand that it starts with letting go of what keeps bringing you pain. You can't keep holding on, waiting for a call, watching them, letting them back into your space, and then wondering why you aren't healing as fast as you would like.

<u>Note to self:</u>
Don't overthink. But don't be naive, either.
9:44 PM.

Overthinking can damage or hinder growth, especially with new relationships. But being naïve or ignoring red flags can cost you severely.

<u>Note to self:</u>
You can let his bullshit stress you out while he is out there living his life, or you can learn from it, and continue with your life.
5:52 AM.

Note to self:
**Honey, you are gold. But, some people prefer silver or bronze, and that's ok.
3:19 AM.**

Stop expecting everyone to see the beauty in you. The one who is for you will see it. Anyone who lost you or didn't realize how special you are was simply not for you. Don't ever think that speaks to your worth.

<u>Note to self:</u>
It didn't work out, and you can't get that time back. Now, stop dwelling on it, and continue with your life. 8:52 PM.

<u>Note to self:</u>
Pretending you don't care won't make it go away. Address your concerns. 2:45 AM.

It's important that you try to find resolutions to your concerns with your partner. Keeping things bottled up and unaddressed only lead to more problems. You can't keep ignoring them, or just sweeping them under the rug. Talk often with your partner. Communication and understanding could save your relationship.

<u>Note to self:</u>
You won't have to convince yourself that he's the one. He'll prove that all on his own.
4:54 PM.

Like the saying goes "when you know, you know". You won't have to try and sell it to yourself. You'll feel it. And that feeling will be hard to ignore.

Note to self:

Make time for the people who make the effort. 9:13 AM.

<u>Note to self:</u>
Make sure you are as high up on their priority list as they are on yours.
10:54 AM.

<u>Note to self:</u>
Reward inconsistency with unavailability.
12:34 PM.

You shouldn't always operate on other people's time. Stop being just something convenient for people. You're worth more than that.

<u>Note to self:</u>
Guard your heart like he
guards his phone.
7:43 AM.

<u>Note to self:</u>
Never fight over a man who didn't care about you enough to not put you in that position with another woman.
9:08 AM.

A man who truly values you will not have you fighting over him. He will never put you in that position. Let the other woman have him, because he has already shown you, with his actions, that he does not value you.

<u>Note to self:</u>
Don't run from love. Run from people who show you their only intention is wasting your time.
4:02 AM.

Watch out for people who seem unsure what they want with you. Or people who are unsure that they even want you. That is usually a clear indicator that they will waste your time.

Note to self:

Yes, you are still a Queen, even without validation from a man.

4:19 PM.

<u>Note to self:</u>
A man does not "complete" you. Let alone, one who isn't even complete, himself.
6:18 AM.

It's nobody's duty to complete you. You are all you need to be complete. You were made whole. A partner is someone to add to everything you already are.

<u>Note to self:</u>
Look for the connection, not just the attraction.
12:14 PM.

Attractive people aren't hard to find. Sex isn't hard to come by. What is in fact rare, is chemistry.

Note to self:

**It's not about long relationships. It's about healthy relationships.
8:19 AM.**

A long lasting relationship is meaningless if it isn't a healthy one.

<u>Note to self:</u>
Stop running back because of sex.
5:41 AM.

Sex is a common reason many people stay attached to toxic people or remain in toxic situations. Either because they are comfortable (sexually) with that person, or they just don't want to add to their "body count", or open themselves up to someone new. In such cases, one must learn to practice self-discipline, or else, they will continue to prolong their healing process.

<u>Note to self:</u>
A lot of men confuse loving a woman with loving how a woman makes them feel.
7:45 PM.

Make sure he's not in it just for the sex. Make sure he is not in it just for the sake of having a woman available to stroke his ego. Men need to get back to loving women, not just using them.

<u>Note to self:</u>
You're not insecure. He just lies too fucking much.
3:51 AM.

Don't let a man who continues to lie, and give you reasons to doubt him convince you that your insecurities are getting the best of you. It's a way of manipulating you into not speaking up, or allowing him to continue to misuse you.

<u>Note to self:</u>
Stop giving unconditional love to people whose loyalty is very conditional.
9:42 AM.

People who are only loyal to you when it's convenient do not deserve your unconditional love. Make sure his loyalty doesn't change when his mood does, or that's not loyalty at all.

<u>Note to self:</u>
People will always make a way to do what it is they truly want to.
4:51 AM.

If he is better at finding excuses than he is with finding a way, then he isn't the one.

<u>Note to self:</u>
Stop repeating yourself. They heard you the first time. They either choose to comply, or they don't.
4:35 AM.

Stop letting people continue to do the same shit over and over again and call it a mistake. It's not. After the first or second time, it becomes a decision. There is no need to keep repeating yourself; because they heard your concerns and they have made a decision that they aren't going to fix the issue. So, you now have a decision to make. Put up with it, or leave.

<u>Note to self:</u>
After you delete their number, delete their pictures from your camera roll as well, so that you don't come across that shit and think it's a sign; It is not.
6:19 AM.

Reminders are the devil when you're trying to move on. Too often, people mistake reminders like old text messages or photos that they may come across as a sign to reach out… it's not. Delete them, and stop looking back.

Note to self:
Stop ignoring the signs and red flags because you like him.
12:43 AM.

I don't care how attractive someone is to you, always pay attention to the signs. Pay attention to their actions, and the things they do that will speak to their character. Ignoring these things because you are too focused on the physical attraction will surely cost you later.

<u>Note to self:</u>
Maybe you hate dating because you keep choosing people you have to raise.
8:14 PM.

Do some self-evaluating. No, you cannot stop men from lying to you, or pretending to be something they are not. However, you can do the best you can to not get involved with the ones who show clear signs of immaturity, toxic or fuck boy behavior.

<u>Note to self:</u>
Stop dealing with men who can't do anything besides fuck you.
4:17 PM.

A woman has no business lying in bed with or committing to a man that will sit there and watch her struggle.

<u>Note to self:</u>
A lot of dudes, these days, just want someone who will be loyal to them while they fuck around. That's what they call a relationship.
7:19 AM.

<u>Note to self:</u>
Finding true love with someone who will respect you and treat you like you deserve will not be easy. But, I promise it'll be worth it.
11:24 AM.

<u>Note to self:</u>
**He doesn't miss you. He just saw that bomb ass picture you posted and is trying to see if he still has access to your loving.
2:47 PM.**

Don't fall for it. Because the moment you let him in, you'll find yourself right back in the situation that you have been trying so hard to get over and away from.

<u>Note to self:</u>
He's mad at your standards because he knows he can't bullshit his way into your life
9:18 AM.

<u>Note to self:</u>
Sometimes, you don't glow because you're in a relationship. Sometimes, you glow because you finally walked away from one.
4:15 PM.

Some people's absence will bring you peace and/or happiness. That is a win.

<u>Note to self:</u>
The harsh reality is that you may just make him better for someone else.
6:25 AM.

People come into our lives for different reasons. Some people will make us better, and some people we will make better. Trying to hold on to someone because of whatever positive influence you feel that you have had on their life, or because of the role you have played in their growth will not make them the one for you. Love doesn't work that way. In life, you might even date some great men/ women who aren't necessarily the one for you. You must learn to accept this truth.

<u>Note to self:</u>
They come and go... and then start begging for another chance.
5:54 PM.

They always seem to come running back. This usually happens when they fail at replacing you.

Note to self:
**It's not your job to fix every man you meet or date that has emotional and trust issues. Save yourself.
2:55 PM.**

You are not a rehabilitation center for damaged men. Because what often happens is, as you are trying to heal them, they are damaging you.

<u>Note to self:</u>
That loyalty hits different when it's mutual.
5:34 PM.

Make sure you're not just out here giving your loyalty away for free.

<u>Note to self:</u>
Just because you're used to him does not mean you need to be with him.
3:13 AM.

You can become used to someone who doesn't deserve you. Always make sure that it is love that's keeping you there, not comfort.

<u>Note to self:</u>
**The truth is in his habits and actions. Ignoring them will be you lying to yourself.
1:47 PM.**

<u>Note to self:</u>
Sometimes, they're not "busy". Sometimes, they are simply just uninterested. 2:52 AM.

Pay attention. When you are a priority, people tend to say things like "I'll make time". But, when you're just an option, or something for convenience, they tend to say things like "if I have time".

<u>Note to self:</u>
Just because someone doesn't lie or cheat does not mean they are not toxic.
4:37 AM.

There are a plethora of other toxic traits. Lying or cheating are not the only ones. Some people are controlling, some are manipulating. Not saying you should run away from everyone who isn't perfect. I'm saying you should learn your partner, and make sure that their "toxic traits" are not as severe, and are things that you can live with.

Note to self:

After you heal and start doing better, make sure you don't go back; because, trust me, they are coming to tempt the fuck out of you. 7:43 AM.

One of the worst things you can do is spend all that time healing yourself, and then hand yourself right back to the person who broke you just because they knew the right things to say.

<u>Note to self:</u>
You either want to move on, or you want to keep fucking him. It cannot be both. 12:34 AM.

Maintaining sexual ties with someone is the best way to prolong your healing process. Don't do it. Its counterproductive, to say the least. Exercise some self-discipline.

<u>Note to self:</u>
Forget how much you think he likes you. He will show you how much he really does or does not by how he prioritizes you.
2:14 PM.

A man who creates time, and finds ways to be an active and consistent part of your life is the one who is truly interested in you.

<u>Note to self:</u>
It's all fun and games until she starts responding to those DMs that she has left unopened because she is done waiting on you.
6:10 PM.

Stop letting men who have made it clear they don't want to be a serious part of your life keep you form exploring your options. If he isn't going to claim you, then you still have the right to entertain who you want. Don't let a man who isn't sure keep you from one who is.

<u>Note to self:</u>
He doesn't miss you. He misses how convenient it was to have you around.
1:02 PM.

Note to self:

Stop making these men feel so entitled to all the second chances that they wouldn't even give you. That's why he keeps doing that same shit.
3:09 AM.

<u>Note to self:</u>
He hasn't changed because you keep running back after every weak ass "I'm sorry, I didn't mean it."
4:36 PM.

Don't be the woman who falls for words, instead of actions. It's easy for a man to figure out what you like to hear, and use those things to continue to string you along or keep you around with no intent on doing right by you.

<u>Note to self:</u>
I promise you, he knows exactly what he did, and he knows it was wrong. He is only making you explain it in attempt to avoid taking responsibility for it.
5:59 PM.

People often try to play dumb to avoid owning their wrong doings. Don't frustrate yourself any further trying to explain something to someone who has made up their mind not to own it.

<u>Note to self:</u>
Nah! Stop trying to use love as an excuse to tolerate all kinds of disrespect.
7:35 PM.

Love is not an excuse to let someone mistreat you. That's not love, sweetheart, that is manipulation. Stop trying to excuse that shit.

<u>Note to self:</u>
I promise you, you can go through hell for a dude and he will still leave you. Stop thinking that is the path to real love.
4:31 PM.

So many women need to unlearn the false notion that, in order to receive the kind of love you deserve, you must first let a man put you through hell.

<u>Note to self:</u>
Consider this— he is making you wait because he knows you will. And he is sleeping around because he knows that you will take him back. This time, prove him wrong.
8:25 AM.

Do not be the woman that he can always come back to after he is done doing all of his dirt. Don't be the woman that is always there. You are doing a disservice to yourself.

<u>Note to self:</u>
For as long as you let him, he will come back. For as long as you allow him, he will use you.
5:23 PM.

Most men would come back again if you let them. Don't mistake that for him being changed or valuing you. It speaks more to your accessibility than it does to his intent to be a better man to you.

<u>Note to self:</u>
Sweetheart, you are wasting the best years of your life on him. Leave now. Save yourself.
4:07 PM.

Know when to say enough is enough. You can't get back the time that you have already spent in a failing or toxic relationship, but you can stop yourself from wasting any more time by staying long after it's over.

<u>Note to self:</u>
You have been proving your loyalty to him for how long, now? When is he going to start proving his to you? 9:13 PM.

Loyalty goes both ways. Respect goes both ways. Only then, is it truly love and a relationship worth being in.

<u>Note to self:</u>
Sometimes, the right choice will hurt like hell.
10:55 AM.

No one ever said it would be easy. But often, it's very much worth it.

<u>Note to self:</u>
Start ignoring men who only text you after 10pm.
1:09 AM.

If he only thinks about you after a certain time, that right there could be a clear indication of what he wants from you.

<u>Note to self:</u>
Those recent and random phone calls and texts from him are just an attempt to give you the minimum so that he can maintain access to you.
7:14 AM.

It's almost like exes can sense when you are on the verge of moving on. Those calls and texts come as a desperate attempt to maintain access to you. Do not allow it.

<u>Note to self:</u>
Sleep well tonight... he's someone else's problem, now.
6:56 AM.

<u>Note to self:</u>
You can put yourself through hell by continuing to be a good woman to the wrong man.
12:44 PM.

Please understand that being a good woman to the wrong man will not turn him into the right man.

Note to self:
Don't let the sex make you forget that he ain't shit. 3:37 PM.

<u>Note to self:</u>
Knowing your worth can get lonely.
2:35 PM.

This is the part that a lot of people struggle with. Self-discipline will play a great role in this area. You'll get tempted. You'll want someone there for the sake of having someone there... But in the end, when the right person does come along, it will make those lonely nights all worth it.

<u>Note to self:</u>
Leaving is not as effective when you keep running back.
7:52 PM.

Learn how to leave and stay gone. When he knows you will always come running back, then nothing changes. You might as well not even have left, in the first place... because you are still very much accessible.

<u>Note to self:</u>
When you have a big heart, you have to be twice as careful.
4:03 AM.

People know how to take advantage of someone's kindness. So, when you are someone who typically goes above and beyond for others, or just have an overall very kind heart, you have to be more mindful of the kind of people you let in your space... because people will use you and be completely unapologetic about it.

<u>Note to self:</u>
Choose single and at peace over being in a miserable relationship.
9:56 AM.

I promise, being single will not kill you. And being in a relationship will not necessarily bring you happiness.

<u>Note to self:</u>
Sometimes, you think you are giving them chances to change, but all you are really doing is giving them more opportunities to disappoint you.
10:46 AM.

Be careful. Every time you forgive someone, and let them back into your life, it can send the message that you will be willing to do so again. Forgiveness is fine. Second chances are ok. But, always know where to draw the line.

<u>Note to self:</u>
Darling, you deserve a man that you don't have to share with other women.
4:12 PM.

Don't let any man convince you that you have to share him with everyone else. You don't. There is a man out there willing to love you and only you.

<u>Note to self:</u>
When you had nothing but
good intentions for
them, the loss is not yours,
it's theirs.
5:19 PM.

<u>Note to self:</u>
I don't want anything I have to question… friendships… "love"… none of it!
4:02 PM.

Anyone who continues to give you reason to question their love and or loyalty is someone you should consider distancing yourself from. When it's real, you won't be uncertain.

<u>Note to self:</u>
**Sometimes, you just have to ask yourself how much longer you want to put up with lies, inconsistency, and apologies that never lead to change.
1:10 PM.**

<u>Note to self:</u>
Put an expiration date on all of that fuck shit you have been tolerating.
2:02 AM.

<u>Note to self:</u>
If he is not sure he wants you, then he does not want you.
7:45 AM.

A man who truly wants you won't leave any room for you to question him or his intentions. Do not wait around for anyone to be sure.

<u>Note to self:</u>
We are done dealing with people who act like they do not care.
6:19 PM.

You don't need to be dealing with anyone who sends mixed signals or people who pretend they don't care. Because, first of all, that is a clear sign of immaturity or some other deeper issues. Secondly, sometimes they really don't care. And you do not need to spend your time trying to figure out if they do or don't. Who has time for that?

<u>Note to self:</u>
Let that hurt go. Do not let them keep that kind of control over your life. 10:23 PM.

When you keep holding on to something someone did to you, it means they still have power over you. Let it go. Take back control over your life, feelings, and mood. Because while you are still being hurt over what they did to you, they are out there living their best life.

<u>Note to self:</u>
Write out that long text message in your notes, but do not copy it into your texts and send it.
He is not worth it.
11:12 PM.

<u>Note to self:</u>
I saw you and felt nothing. That was the ultimate win 2:44 AM.

The ultimate win is not revenge. The ultimate win is happiness. It's being truly and completely over it, to the point you are no longer affected by the thought or sight of the person who hurt you.

Note to self:
Sometimes, you're not even mad that it's over; you're just upset that you fell for another bullshit ass dude, in the first place, and wasted your time.
1:09 AM.

<u>Note to self:</u>
This time, listen to your friends and let him go!
9:55 AM.

Sometimes, your friends are right. Sometimes, It's hard for you to see how fucked up an individual truly is because of all the feelings you have invested in that person.

Note to self:
Don't just be something convenient. Be someone valued, and wanted.
12:34 PM.

<u>Note to self:</u>
Dear Queen, stop chasing him, and let him court you. 4:22 PM.

You shouldn't be chasing any man, period! You, My Dear, are the prize!

<u>Note to self:</u>
It's ok to admit that you're not ok.
6:19 PM.

Even strong women are allowed to be fed up. You are allowed to be tired. You are allowed to be emotional. You are allowed to be hurt, disappointed, and whatever else you may feel. You are human.

<u>Note to self:</u>
You deserve disrespectful sex from a respectful man. 2:59 AM.

Note to self:

Time will heal you... but not when you keep going back. 12:07 PM.

<u>Note to self:</u>
Save all that loyalty and good sex for someone who's going to reciprocate that energy.
1:44 PM.

<u>Note to self:</u>
What you allow, you condone.
9:14 AM.

When you stay and complain over and over again about how you are being treated, all it does is send the message that you don't have it in you to leave… and that is a dangerous message to send someone because it gives them all the leverage.

<u>Note to self:</u>
You can't change people,
but you can change how
you deal with them and how
much you invest in them.
8:12 AM.

<u>Note to self:</u>
Make sure you reflect on yourself as well. It's not always them.
12:22 PM.

We probably all have toxic traits. Obviously not all are as severe as others. However, you should figure out what you may need to work on, and work on it, because not everyone is going to put up with the excuses, or you blaming it on your zodiac sign or saying things like "that's just how I am".

<u>Note to self:</u>
He knew what he was doing.
He also knew how forgiving
you are. ...and that's what
he was counting on.
9:55 AM.

Be careful not to have your kind heart
get taken advantage of.

<u>Note to self:</u>
A man will tell a woman he isn't ready for anything serious but still expect her to commit to him.
6:10 AM.

<u>Note to self:</u>
You shouldn't have to teach a grown man what it means to be faithful and or loyal. 8:14 AM.

<u>Note to self:</u>
When a man really loves you, making you happy will make him happy.
7:02 PM.

This speaks to how much a man truly values you. One who shares your moods with you. One who wants to make you happy, because seeing you filled with joy brings joy to him. One who does not want to hurt you, because it will also hurt him.

<u>Note to self:</u>
You're giving him power by still paying attention to him. 4:39: AM.

<u>Note to self:</u>
This time, when you tell him you're done, be done. Because, at this point, he doesn't believe you.
12:12 AM.

The fact that you keep going back or threatening to leave without really leaving only lets him know that he has you... that he can continue to do as he pleases, and you will always be there.

<u>Note to self:</u>
Sometimes, you'll have to
let go of a man you don't
want to let go of, in order
to create space for the man
you've been praying for.
4:17 PM.

<u>Note to self:</u>
Stop stalking his social media. I promise, that shit isn't helping you heal.
12:56 AM.

You are only impeding your healing process by watching and concerning yourself with their every move. The only person being hurt by that is you. The only person whose mood changes is yours. Stop watching him and focus on you. Let that hope go. Let that hurt go.

<u>Note to self:</u>
**Choose happiness over history.
4:11 AM.**

<u>Note to self:</u>
Make sure you're happy in real life.
12:12 PM.

<u>Note to self:</u>
Keep curving these men until one really speaks to your soul.
1:09 PM.

<u>Note to self:</u>
Knowing when to say "fuck it, it's his loss" is a very important part of self care. 2:39 PM.

Note to self:
I don't care how lonely you get, leave his ass blocked! 1:01 AM.

<u>Note to self:</u>
That potential you see in everyone is what keeps fucking you up.
9:16 AM.

Note to self:

Just because you want him to does not mean he has changed.
4:22 AM.

Note to self:
It's ok to start over. It beats staying and being miserable.
8:29 PM.

<u>Note to self:</u>
He is very replaceable.
3:23 PM.

Stop letting men who do the very minimum to keep you act as if they are the best thing since sliced bread. Men who do the minimum aren't hard to come by. Forget being able to just replace him, there is even plenty of room for an upgrade.

Lightning Source UK Ltd.
Milton Keynes UK
UKHW011123161219
355473UK00001B/67/P

9 781977 215789